Henry Ford
Father of the Auto Industry

JOSH GREGORY

Children's Press®
An Imprint of Scholastic Inc.
New York Toronto London Auckland Sydney
Mexico City New Delhi Hong Kong
Danbury, Connecticut

Content Consultant
James Marten, PhD
Professor and Chair, History Department
Marquette University
Milwaukee, Wisconsin

Library of Congress Cataloging-in-Publication Data
Gregory, Josh.
Henry Ford / Josh Gregory.
pages cm.—(A true book)
Audience: Grade 4 to 6.
Includes bibliographical references and index.
ISBN 978-0-531-24777-8 (lib. bdg.) — ISBN 978-0-531-28463-6 (paperback)
1. Ford, Henry, 1863-1947 —Juvenile literature. 2. Automobile engineers —United States —
Biography —Juvenile literature. 3. Inventors —United States —Biography —Juvenile literature.
4. Industrialists —United States —Biography —Juvenile literature. 5. Automobile industry and
trade —United States —History —Juvenile literature. I. Title.
TL140.F6G74 2013
338.7'629222092—dc23[B]   2013000098

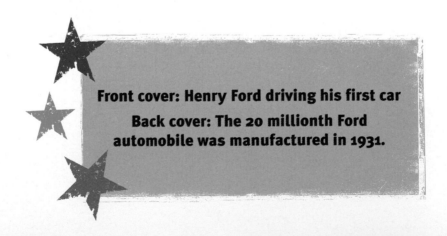

Front cover: Henry Ford driving his first car

Back cover: The 20 millionth Ford automobile was manufactured in 1931.

Find the Truth!

Everything you are about to read is true *except* for one of the sentences on this page.

Which one is **TRUE**?

T or F   Henry Ford invented the automobile.

T or F   Henry Ford's first car was called the quadricycle.

Find the answers in this book.

Contents

THE **BIG** TRUTH!

Henry Ford rolls his first working automobile, the quadricycle, from his workshop.

4 Later Years

How did the Great Depression affect Ford's business? 35

The first Ford Model A was purchased by Dr. Ernst Pfenning of Chicago, Illinois.

Henry Ford restored his childhood home after his parents died. It was later moved to nearby Greenfield Village, Michigan.

CHAPTER 1

From Dearborn to Detroit

On July 30, 1863, William and Mary Ford gave birth to a son. They named him Henry. The Fords were farmers just outside of Dearborn, Michigan, about 8 miles (13 kilometers) west of Detroit. They raised their eight children, including young Henry, to work hard at the family business. They could not have imagined that their son would one day change the world.

Henry Ford was born at home on his family's farm.

A Different Time

The world of Henry's childhood was very different from the one he would help create. When he was born, cars did not exist. Horses were the most common form of transportation. Machines were often simple compared to what exists today. Their power was provided not by an engine, but by horses, water, wind, or the people using them.

When Henry Ford was a child, farmers used horse-drawn equipment.

Henry was a little more than two years old when this photo was taken.

Interested Early On

Henry took an early interest in machines. As a child, he liked to take his toys apart to see how they worked. He eventually began building simple inventions of his own.

In 1876, when Henry was 12 years old, his father took him along on a trip to Detroit. There, the boy saw a cart powered by a steam engine. Amazed by the machine, he approached its owner to ask how it worked. After explaining, the owner let Henry steer the cart himself.

In the 1880s, Detroit was known for manufacturing stoves.

Walking to Work

After Henry's experience with the steam-powered cart, he couldn't get machines off his mind. When he was 16, he left home and school and walked to Detroit. From that point forward, his education came from hands-on experience. Henry searched for a job that would let him work with machines and learn more about them. He worked at various machine shops in the city. In his spare time, he continued tinkering with his own inventions.

An Education in Engines

Within a year, Ford had gained enough experience to earn a position at the Detroit Dry Dock Company, which built ships. There, he soon became an expert in steam engines.

Around the same time, he also learned about **internal combustion engines**. These engines were powered by gasoline. He was intrigued by the new invention but still preferred to work with steam engines.

Toward the end of the 1800s, steam engines were used to power a variety of machines, including oceangoing ships.

Back to the Farm

After three years in Detroit, Ford returned to Dearborn and worked at his family's farm once again. He did not give up his passion for building things, though. He soon got a job at the Westinghouse Engine Company, which built steam-powered engines. Ford repaired and operated the company's engines for local farmers. He also demonstrated how the engines could be used to power farm machines.

Steam-powered plows and tractors became more common toward the end of the 1800s.

12

A showman named Achille Philion built the steam-powered Philion Road Carriage in 1892. He only made one. It was one of the first cars built in the United States.

The Horseless Carriage

While working for Westinghouse, Ford set up a small machine shop at his family's farm. He also began planning a steam-powered "horseless carriage." Experimenting with different designs, he soon decided steam engines were too dangerous for such a vehicle. Steam engines require a large amount of pressure inside the engines to make them work. As a result, they have a high risk of exploding. Ford began to think that an internal combustion engine was exactly what he needed.

Ford sometimes called his wife, Clara, his "great believer."

Starting a Family

In 1885, Ford met a woman named Clara Jane Bryant. Clara had grown up on a farm in southern Michigan, just as Ford had. The two began seeing each other, and they were married in 1888. In September 1891, Ford brought his wife with him when he moved back to Detroit. Once again, he hoped to find a job that would teach him valuable new **engineering** skills.

This time, Ford wanted to study electricity. He got a job with Detroit's electricity provider, the Edison Illuminating Company. A fast learner and a natural with mechanical devices, Ford quickly moved up through the company.

On November 6, 1893, Ford's family welcomed a new addition. Clara gave birth to their first and only child, a son named Edsel.

Henry Ford (left) was friends with Thomas Edison (right), founder of the Edison Illuminating Company.

Ford worked many long hours
in a shed at home to build a
working engine and automobile.

On the Road

In December 1893, Ford was promoted at Edison to the position of chief engineer. The job did not have regular hours. Instead, he could be called in at any time to fix an electrical problem. This left him with plenty of time to work on his own inventions. By the end of the month, he had completed a working internal combustion engine.

 Ford had to break down part of the wall around his workshop's door to fit his first car through.

Putting the Engine to Use

Inspired by the work of other car inventors of the time, Ford began looking for a way to use his new engine to power a horseless carriage. In 1896, he finally completed his first working car. He called it the quadricycle, because it was built using four bicycle wheels. The car could go as fast as 20 miles per hour (32 kph).

Ford sits proudly on his new invention, the quadricycle.

Early Innovators

Henry Ford was an early **innovator** in automobile manufacturing, but he was not the first to build a gasoline-powered car. More than 10 years before Ford built his quadricycle, Karl Benz created a three-wheeled car (below) in Germany. In early 1896, brothers Frank and Charles Duryea of Massachusetts became the first people in the United States to build a gas-powered car.

Ford was an independent thinker who preferred to do things his own way.

Ford's First Sales

Word of Ford's new car spread across Detroit. Local investors offered to provide Ford with the money he needed to start a car company. With their funding, he quit his job at Edison in 1899 and formed the Detroit Automobile Company. His company's first car was released in 1900. Ford was unhappy with the results, however, and wanted to improve the design. The investors pressured him to work on a new model instead.

Unhappy with this pressure, Ford turned his attention away from the company and began building race cars. As his speedy cars won race after race, Ford was soon convinced he had the knowledge to build the truly great vehicles he had always dreamed of building. He decided to form a new company that could compete with the other car manufacturers that had sprung up in recent years.

Ford stands with racing driver Barney Oldfield (seated) by Ford's "Old 99" race car.

The Ford Motor Company designed, tested, and built early Ford cars at the Ford Piquette Avenue Plant in Detroit.

CHAPTER 3

A Car for Everyone

In 1902, Ford left the Detroit Automobile Company, which had been renamed the Henry Ford Company. The next year, he formed the Ford Motor Company and began selling a car called the Model A. The Model A was simple and well built. It became known for being reliable and needing repairs less often than its competitors.

By 1909, there were more than 200 car manufacturers in the United States.

Long Hours

The Model A was a reasonable success. Ford sold 215 cars in the first two months and about 1,000 in the first year. Success didn't stop Ford from working hard to improve the model. He and his employees sometimes worked as many as 16 hours a day, every day of the week. At first, they could build only a few cars each day. Ford found better, faster ways to build car as time went on. Two years after launching the Model A, the company could produce 25 cars per day.

The Ford Motor Company sold its first Model A on July 15, 1903.

Inventor George Selden (driving) patented his internal combustion engine design before selling the patent to ALAM.

Legal Trouble

Ford ran into problems during the company's early days. The Association of Licensed Automobile Manufacturers (ALAM) held a **patent** on gas-powered cars. It required all U.S. car manufacturers to pay ALAM for a license. Ford argued that it was unfair for one group to patent something that many people had contributed to. He refused to pay. ALAM brought a **lawsuit** against Ford. Though Ford eventually won the case, the process took almost 10 years.

The Model T made cars affordable to everyone, not just the wealthy.

The Universal Car

In 1908, Ford released a new car called the Model T.
Unlike most cars of the time, the Model T was
designed for everyday, working-class people
to purchase. With a simpler design and a more
efficient production method, Ford was able to
sell the car at an extremely low price. Many cars
available at the time cost more than $2,000. The
Model T cost $850 in 1908, and the price dropped
below $300 over the next 20 years.

A Changing World

Ford's plan to sell cars at a low price was a huge success. The company sold more than 10,000 Model Ts in the first year. Beginning in 1909, it offered no other models.

Inexpensive cars changed American life permanently. Highways began to be built across the country, and people stopped using horses for transportation. With fast, easy travel available to more people, cities grew and **suburbs** quickly expanded outward.

Replacing horses with cars solved sanitation problems caused by horse waste in city streets.

Cars and pedestrians pack State Street in downtown Chicago, Illinois.

Low Prices, High Sales

In order to make a profit selling such inexpensive cars, Ford had to sell a huge number of vehicles. As a result, the company grew rapidly. When the Model T was introduced in 1908, the company employed about 2,000 people. Three years later, that number had doubled, and the company was producing around 35,000 cars each year. In 1913, Ford opened a huge new factory built to produce Model Ts at an even faster rate.

Timeline of Ford and His Company

July 30, 1863
Henry Ford is born.

1896
Ford successfully completes the quadricycle, his first car.

On the Line

The new factory used a process called mass production. Employees worked on an assembly line. Machines brought the pieces needed, and the workers performed the same task all day. Each task was one step in assembling a car. For example, one worker might attach the left front wheel to every car on the line. Each car would then move to the next employee in line, who attached the next wheel, and so on, until the car was complete.

1913
Construction of a new, assembly-line-based factory is completed.

1903
The Ford Motor Company is created; the first Model A is sold.

1908
The Model T is released; production of the Model A stops.

Wages and Benefits

Mass production allowed Ford to produce more cars and lower its prices at the same time. It also made the process so efficient that he could afford to pay his workers more while reducing the number of hours they worked. In 1914, he began paying all of his employees a minimum of five dollars per day. This was more than twice the average wage at other automobile manufacturers.

A Model T is dropped into place at its next station on the assembly line.

By the 1920s, the Ford Motor Company employed thousands of workers from a variety of backgrounds.

Ford began offering other benefits to his workers. A large number of them were **immigrants** who did not speak English. Some could not read or write. Ford began offering free classes to help these workers learn to write, speak, and read English. In return, he required them to work hard and follow all company rules whether they were at home or at work. Some people complained that he was too strict. Others praised his generosity.

Many Models

Under Henry Ford's leadership, the Ford Motor Company designed and manufactured many different models of cars over the years. Some offered minor improvements on previous models, while others were packed with brand-new features.

Model A (1903)

On July 15, 1903, the Ford Motor Company made its first sale when Dr. Ernst Pfenning of Chicago, Illinois, purchased a Model A. This early Ford model was sometimes called the Fordmobile. It had no roof or windshield and could reach speeds of around 30 miles per hour (48 kph).

Model T (1908)

Between October 1, 1908, and May 26, 1927, Ford manufactured more than 15 million Model Ts. The Model T was designed so almost anyone could afford and maintain it. Ford himself called it "the universal car." The Model T's popularity made the Ford Motor Company the biggest automobile manufacturer in the world.

Model A (1927)

In 1927, Ford replaced the Model T with a new car, the Model A. Though it shared a name with the company's very first design, there was no mistaking the two models. The newer Model A came in several different styles. Some had soft-top convertible roofs and four seats, while others had hard tops and storage areas in the back.

Ford took full ownership of the
Ford Motor Company in the 1910s.

DEMONSTRATION
2-385-19
N.Y. 19

Later Years

As the Ford Motor Company made more money, Henry Ford continued to invest all of the profits in growing the company. This displeased the company's **stockholders**. They wanted him to share the profits as **dividends** instead. As always, Ford did not like having to answer to other people. He decided to buy the stockholders' shares in the company. By 1919, after paying around $100 million, Ford owned 100 percent of the company.

Ford's stockholders included John and Horace Dodge, who began their own automobile company in 1910.

Going Vertical

In 1918, Ford made his son, Edsel, president of the company. However, Ford largely continued to run things behind the scenes. He began working on vertical integration. This meant that instead of buying materials from other companies, the Ford Motor Company would have its own rubber plantations, sawmills, and mines to provide the resources needed for building cars. The company soon had its own railroad and ships to transport these materials. This allowed Ford to cut costs even more.

Henry Ford (left) looks over the drawing of a car design with his assistant, John Wandersee (center), and son, Edsel (right).

The new Model A caught the attention of many people who had long been waiting for improvements on the Model T's design.

A New Model

By the late 1920s, the Model T was starting to seem out-of-date compared to other cars that were available. Ford was reluctant to change or replace the Model T. But eventually he realized the company needed to change to keep up with the competition. In 1927, the company stopped making Model Ts and started making a new Model A. It included many features that car buyers wanted, such as the ability to be driven at higher speeds.

People who could not afford food sometimes waited for hours in long, crowded breadlines during the Great Depression.

Troubled Times

The Model A was successful but did not sell as well as the Model T had. One reason was the collapse of the economy in 1929. During this period, known as the Great Depression, many people lost their jobs and did not have money to buy extras such as cars. Even the Ford Motor Company was forced to lay off many of its workers and cut wages for those who kept their jobs.

Dealing With the Unions

During the Great Depression, the Ford Motor Company began having conflicts with unions. In 1935, the Wagner Act gave workers the right to unionize and negotiate for better pay and benefits from company owners. Ford was against unions. He believed that he treated his employees fairly already, and he did not like others telling him what to do. He tried to stop his employees from unionizing but was eventually forced to allow the unions to exist.

Ford workers sometimes went on strike, or stopped working, as they negotiated with the company.

World War II

In 1939, World War II broke out in Europe. Though he did not personally believe in war, Ford soon made a deal to manufacture airplane engines for the United States and its allies. In 1941, he opened a massive new factory called Willow Run. There, the company mass-produced bomber planes. Ford's planes helped the Allies win the war in 1945.

Henry Ford worked with his son, Edsel, on planning the Willow Run factory.

A Pacifist at War

Ford considered himself a **pacifist**. He was against U.S. involvement in World War I (1914–1918) and World War II. In 1915, he even sponsored a "Peace Ship," a failed expedition to find a peaceful end to World War I. In spite of this, Ford produced tons of war supplies during both world wars. This contradiction has led some historians to doubt his pacifism. Others have argued that Ford made an exception to support his country.

Henry and Clara Ford were photographed riding in Ford's quadricycle not long after his retirement.

Family Business

In 1943, in the middle of the war, Edsel Ford died of stomach cancer at the age of 49. Henry Ford was devastated by his son's early death. In addition, he found himself once again president of his company. However, his health was failing as well. He had suffered two strokes and often acted strangely, which strained his business relationships. Finally, in 1945, Ford was forced to retire from his beloved company. His grandson, Henry Ford II, took over as president.

End of an Era

On the night of April 7, 1947, Ford died at home of bleeding in his brain.

Henry Ford was one of the greatest inventors and businessmen in American history. His ideas revolutionized manufacturing and brought cars into the garages of everyday people. Thousands of people gathered for his funeral. Decades later, he is still remembered as the man who changed the way we travel. ★

Ford Motor Company plants closed down for the day of Ford's funeral.

True Statistics

Number of Model Ts sold: More than 15 million

Cost of a Model T in 1908: $850

Cost of a Model T in 1924: $260

Top speed of the original Model A: 30 mph (48 kph)

Top speed of Ford's quadricycle: 20 mph (32 kph)

Number of Ford employees in 1908: Around 2,000

Number of Ford employees in 1911: Around 4,000

Minimum wage for Ford employees in 1914: $5 per day

Did you find the truth?

F Henry Ford invented the automobile.

T Henry Ford's first car was called the quadricycle.

Resources

Books

Mitchell, Don. *Driven: A Photobiography of Henry Ford*. Washington, DC: National Geographic, 2010.

Venezia, Mike. *Henry Ford: Big Wheel in the Auto Industry*. New York: Children's Press, 2009.

Zuehlke, Jeffrey. *Henry Ford*. Minneapolis: Lerner Publications, 2007.

Visit this Scholastic Web site for more information on Henry Ford:
★ www.factsfornow.scholastic.com
Enter the keywords **Henry Ford**

Important Words

dividends (DIV-uh-dendz) — shares of the money earned by an investment or a business

efficient (i-FISH-uhnt) — working very well and not wasting time or money

engineering (en-juh-NEER-ing) — designing and building machines or structures

immigrants (IM-uh-gruhnts) — people who move from one country to another and settle there permanently

innovator (IN-uh-vay-tur) — someone who has new ideas or creates new inventions

internal combustion engines (in-TUR-nuhl kuhm-BUS-chuhn EN-jinz) — engines that are powered by burning gasoline

lawsuit (LAW-soot) — a court case brought by one person or company against another

pacifist (PAS-uh-fust) — a person who strongly and actively opposes conflict, especially war

patent (PAT-uhnt) — a legal document that gives an inventor the right to make or profit from an invention

stockholders (STAHK-hol-durz) — people who own shares, or stock, in a company

suburbs (SUHB-urbz) — areas near the outer edge of a city; a suburb is made up mostly of homes, with few businesses

Index

Page numbers in **bold** indicate illustrations

About the Author

Josh Gregory writes and edits books for kids. He lives in Chicago, Illinois.